THE
PIGS IN
BLANKETS
cookbook

THE
PIGS IN
BLANKETS
cookbook

50 BACON & SAUSAGE SHOWSTOPPERS
(NOT JUST FOR CHRISTMAS)

THE JOLLY HOG

EBURY
PRESS

FOREWORD

Whoever decided to wrap a piece of streaky bacon around a sausage is, in our eyes, a god! This cookbook has one purpose and one purpose only – to celebrate the Pig in Blanket. Or the PIB, as we fondly call it.

What was known as a festive treat that compliments the turkey is now a lot more than that, as you will discover in this book. These recipes span the seasons from summery lettuce cups to an extremely indulgent festive fondue.

This book is brought to you by The Jolly Hog, a bunch of meat-obsessive brothers based in Bristol. The Jolly Hog was started by professional rugby player Olly Kohn and his brothers Josh and Max. What started off with a small sausage machine and an events business selling sausages is now a meat brand that can be found in major supermarkets.

The Jolly Hog outdoor-bred PIBS are made with dry-cured, double-smoked, black-treacle bacon and the sausage meat is coarsely ground and seasoned with sage.

We hope you love and enjoy making these recipes as much as we do.

Olly, Max & Josh
The Jolly Hog

CONTENTS

CHRISTMAS

PIBS
TRIFLE

What could be a better recipe for Christmas than a savoury pigs-in-blankets trifle?! Combining two of the signature foods of Christmas – trifle and pigs in blankets – this crazy food idea doesn't just look epic, but also tastes amazing.

SERVES: 4–6
PREP TIME: 20 minutes
COOK TIME: 30 minutes

FOR THE CRANBERRY SAUCE
150g light muscovado sugar
100ml Cointreau
400g fresh or frozen cranberries
sea salt

FOR THE CANDIED BACON
6 The Jolly Hog Smoked Rashers Streaky Bacon
2 tbsp brown sugar
2 tbsp orange juice

FOR THE TRIFLE
250g brioche, cut into chunks
sea salt
1.5kg potatoes, peeled and chopped into chunks
30 The Jolly Hog Pigs in Blankets
50g butter
200ml cream
small bunch of watercress, to garnish

1 Put the sugar and Cointreau into a large, heavy-bottomed saucepan. Bring to a simmer and allow to bubble until the sugar has dissolved. Add the cranberries to the pan with a pinch of salt and stir well. Return to the boil and cook for 10 minutes or until the sauce starts to thicken.

2 In the meantime, put the bacon into a frying pan over a medium heat and cook for 7–8 minutes until it's just done but not crisped. Transfer to a plate lined with paper towels.

3 Put the sugar and orange juice into the frying pan. Stir over a gentle heat until the sugar has dissolved, then turn up the heat and return the bacon to the pan. Cook, turning the bacon regularly until it is browned and caramelised. Transfer to a plate to cool.

4 Scatter half of the brioche over the bottom of a deep trifle bowl. Pour over half of the cranberry sauce, then put the remaining bread into the cranberry pan and stir. Set aside for the sauce to soak into the bread.

5 Bring a large saucepan of water to the boil. Add some salt and the potato chunks and bring it back to the boil. Simmer for 10 minutes until the potato is very tender.

6 While the potatoes are cooking, heat a large frying pan and cook the pigs in blankets for 5–8 minutes until browned all over and cooked through.

7 When the potatoes are cooked, drain well, then return to the hot pan along with the butter and cream, and season well with salt and pepper. Mash until completely smooth. Keep warm.

8 When all of the elements are ready, lay half of the pigs in blankets on top of the brioche in the bowl. Add the remaining soaked brioche and then the rest of the pigs in blankets, reserving 4 or 5 for decoration.

9 Spoon or pipe the mashed potato on top of the trifle and decorate with the candied bacon and, remaining pigs in blankets, watercress and serve warm.

9

PUFF PASTRY PIBS & CHRISTMAS CAMEMBERT WREATH

with Speedy Festive Chutney

A great festive centrepiece. We've ramped up a traditional baked Camembert with pastry-wrapped pigs in blankets for dipping. There is also a super-speedy, full-flavoured festive chutney that can easily be whipped up while your Camembert and sausages bake in the oven.

MAKES: 1 wreath
PREP TIME: 10 minutes
COOK TIME: 25 minutes

FOR THE WREATH

- 500g block of puff pastry
- flour, for dusting
- 20 The Jolly Hog Pigs in Blankets
- 1 egg, lightly whisked
- ½ tbsp black sesame seeds
- ½ tbsp white sesame seeds
- 250g Camembert wheel, in wooden box
- fresh rosemary, to serve

FOR THE CHUTNEY

- 1 small red onion, finely diced
- 1 tbsp salted butter
- 1 tbsp dried mixed herbs
- 1 tbsp mixed spice
- 80g currants or raisins
- 50g dried apricots
- 100g dried figs
- 100ml balsamic vinegar
- 60g soft brown sugar
- 100ml water

You will need a 20cm cake tin.

1 Preheat the oven to 200°C/180°C fan/gas mark 6. Line a large baking tray with greaseproof paper.

2 Roll out the puff pastry on a lightly floured surface and cut out a circle roughly 28cm in diameter. Transfer to the lined baking tray.

3 Place a 20cm cake tin in the centre of the pastry circle and cut 12 lines from the edge of the cake tin to the edge of the circle to create 12 sections, like a clock.

4 Place one pig in blanket diagonally on each pastry section and roll up towards the cake tin. Working your way round the clock, repeat until 12 sausages are wrapped in the puff pastry.

5 Brush each sausage roll with a little of the whisked egg. Sprinkle over the black and white sesame seeds.

6 Unwrap the Camembert and place it (still in its wooden casing) in the centre of the cake tin. Place the spare pigs in blankets in the cake tin around the cheese and bake in the oven for 25 minutes.

7 In the meantime, make the chutney. Place the red onion in a heavy-bottomed saucepan along with the butter. Gently fry the onion over a medium heat for 4–5 minutes until it begins to soften.

8 Add the dried mixed herbs and mixed spice to the pan and continue to cook for a further 1 minute. Add the currants or raisins, apricots and figs to the pan and pour in the balsamic vinegar.

9 Sprinkle in the sugar and stir all the ingredients together. Pour in the water and bring to a simmer. Allow to gently simmer for 15–20 minutes until the fruit has softened and the liquid reduced. Once thickened, remove from the heat and allow the chutney to cool and further thicken.

10 Remove the cake tin from the oven and place it and the puff pastry pigs on a serving board.

11 Add the cooked spare pigs in blankets to the top of the Camembert. Spoon the cooled chutney into the cake tin around the edge of the baked Camembert. Finish with a little fresh rosemary and serve.

MINI HERBY HOGS IN HOLES

with Dijonaise

These little toad-in-the-holes are ideal for a savoury snack, kids' lunchboxes or alternative party nibbles.

MAKES: 10
PREP TIME: 5 minutes
COOK TIME: 25 minutes

2 tbsp rapeseed oil
10 The Jolly Hog Pigs
  in Blankets

FOR THE BATTER
2 medium free-range
  eggs
100g plain flour
100ml milk
sea salt and black pepper
1 tbsp dried mixed herbs

TO SERVE
fresh rosemary leaves
2 tbsp Dijonaise

You will need a 12-hole
  muffin tin.

1 Preheat the oven to 220°C/200°C fan/gas mark 7.

2 Place a dash of oil and a pig in blanket in each of the 10 holes of the muffin tin. Put the tin in the oven and roast for 5 minutes.

3 While the sausage begins to cook, make the batter: crack the eggs into a large jug and then sift in the flour. Whisk together to form a thick paste and then pour in the milk. Whisk until a smooth, thick batter forms.

4 Season the batter with salt and pepper and then sprinkle in the mixed herbs – whisk again to combine.

5 After the sausages have been cooking for 5 minutes and the oil is sizzling, carefully but quickly remove the tin from the oven and gently pour the batter into each hole around the sausages. Return the tin to the oven as quickly as possible and bake for 15–20 minutes until the batter has risen and turned golden, then remove.

6 Remove the mini toad-in-the-holes from the tin and place on a serving plate with a scattering of rosemary and a bowl of Dijonaise for dipping.

12

- 1 tbsp salted butter
- 1 banana shallot, finely sliced
- 5 The Jolly Hog Pigs in Blankets, roughly chopped
- 400g sprouts, finely shredded
- 1 tbsp fresh or dried thyme
- sea salt and black pepper

1 In a large, wide frying pan, melt the butter over a medium heat. Add the shallot and gently fry for 2–3 minutes.

2 Add the pigs in blankets to the pan and fry for 3 minutes. Add the sprouts and fry for 3–4 minutes, stirring occasionally and allowing the sprouts to brown a little.

3 Just before serving, sprinkle through the thyme and season with salt and pepper.

PIBS & SHREDDED SPROUTS

Pimp up this classic Christmas side by combining two festive classics in one delightful dish!

SERVES: 4 (as a side)
PREP TIME: 5 minutes
COOK TIME: 10 minutes

13

PIBS, CRANBERRY & DEEP-FRIED BRIE SALAD

with Toasted Pecans

What better way to enjoy a salad than topping it with little sausages and oozy, melty deep-fried cheese? Add a sticky, sweet cranberry dressing and toasted nuts and it's a vibrant salad that can be devoured all year round.

SERVES: 4
PREP TIME: 10 minutes
COOK TIME: 25 minutes

FOR THE SALAD
10 The Jolly Hog Pigs in Blankets
140g salad leaves
60g good-quality dried cranberries
50g pecans, toasted

FOR THE BRIE
50g plain flour
2 medium free-range eggs, lightly whisked
85g panko breadcrumbs
200g brie (ideally round), cut into 8 equal wedges
1 litre vegetable oil, for deep-frying

FOR THE DRESSING
20g cranberry sauce
1 tbsp maple syrup
1 tbsp wholegrain mustard
1 tbsp rapeseed oil
sea salt and black pepper

1 Preheat the oven to 200°C/180°C fan/gas mark 6.

2 Place the pigs in blankets in a roasting tin and roast in the oven for 25 minutes.

3 In the meantime, place the flour, eggs and breadcrumbs in three separate, shallow bowls.

4 First coat a piece of brie in flour, knocking off any excess, then place in the egg bowl and completely coat. Allow any excess egg to drip off, then finally place in the breadcrumbs, patting them gently to ensure they stick to the brie. Place the breadcrumb-coated brie back into the egg and then back into the breadcrumbs for a second coat. Set aside until ready to fry and repeat with the remaining wedges.

5 When ready to fry, pour the oil into a large, heavy-bottomed saucepan and place over a medium–high heat. To test the oil is hot enough, carefully place a cube of stale bread in the oil and if it instantly sizzles and starts to turn golden, the oil is ready.

6 Carefully lower the brie wedges into the oil and fry for 2–3 minutes until totally golden – you may want to do this in batches to ensure the oil stays hot.

Once golden, remove the wedges using a slotted spoon and place on paper towels to remove any excess oil.

7 Make the dressing by placing all the ingredients in a small bowl or mug and gently whisking together. If a thinner dressing is desired, simply add a small dash of water.

8 When ready to serve, place the salad leaves in a large bowl or serving platter. Dot over the cooked pigs in blankets and fried brie. Sprinkle over the dried cranberries and toasted pecans, breaking some up in your hands for a range of texture.

9 Finish the salad with the dressing and serve.

15

10 The Jolly Hog Pigs
  in Blankets
2 Jolly Cow burgers
2 brioche burger buns
100g brie, cut into
  4 thick slices
2 tbsp chilli jam, plus
  extra to serve

20g rocket
2 tbsp garlic mayonnaise
French fries, to serve

You will need 2 wooden
  skewers (optional).

PIBS BURGER

with Melty Brie, Chilli Jam & Garlic Mayo

Out of the way patties, here comes the ultimate PIBS burger! With melty, oozy brie, sweet chilli jam and punchy garlic mayo, this sausage-style burger is an absolute game-changer.

1 Preheat the oven to 200°C/180°C fan/gas mark 6.

2 Place the pigs in blankets in a roasting tin and roast in the oven for 25 minutes. Once the pigs in blankets are cooked, remove from the oven.

3 In the meantime, cook the burgers as per the packet instructions

4 Slice the brioche buns in half and load the bottom half of the buns with the sausages. Lay two slices of brie over the top of the sausages in each bun. Place the loaded buns and bun tops under a hot grill for 2 minutes until the brie has melted and the bun tops are toasted.

5 Remove the buns from the grill. Spoon over the chilli jam and top with the rocket leaves. Spread the garlic mayo on the top bun and place on top. Use a small wooden skewer to hold your burger together, if required.

6 Serve alongside French fries and extra chilli jam.

MAKES: 2
PREP TIME: 10 minutes
COOK TIME: 25 minutes

17

PIBS
FESTIVE
BREAD BOWL
FONDUE

Great for any party
or festive gathering,
this fabulous fondue is
a fun way to enjoy any
leftover Christmas pigs
in blankets.

SERVES: 4
PREP TIME: 5 minutes
COOK TIME: 30 minutes

10 The Jolly Hog Pigs
   in Blankets
1 circular or cob loaf
250ml good-quality dry
   white wine
1 tsp lemon juice
1 tsp cornflour
200g Gruyère, grated
200g Emmental, grated
black pepper

TO SERVE
1 pack of cured meat
1 jar of cornichons

You will need fondue
   skewers.

1 Preheat the oven to 200°C/180°C fan/gas mark 6.

2 Place the pigs in blankets in a roasting tin and
roast in the oven for 25 minutes.

3 Carve the top off the cob loaf. Pull out the centre
of the bread to create a hollow bowl and cut the
removed bread into chunks. Place the hollowed loaf
and bread chunks on a baking tray and place in the
oven for 5 minutes.

4 Pour the wine and lemon juice into a heavy-
bottomed pan over a medium heat and bring to the
boil. Simmer for 1 minute.

5 Whisk in the cornflour before turning down
the heat to low and sprinkling in both cheeses.
Continuously stir until the cheese has melted and
a smooth, stringy consistency is achieved.

6 Pour the fondue into the warmed bread and finish
with a little black pepper.

7 Serve alongside the cooked pigs in blankets, toast
chunks, cured meat and cornichons.

20 The Jolly Hog Pigs
in Blankets
1 tbsp rapeseed oil
3 large free-range eggs
150g plain flour
225ml milk
1 tbsp dried mixed herbs
sea salt and black pepper
seasonal greens, to serve

FOR THE GRAVY
1 small red onion,
finely sliced
1 tbsp salted butter
1 tbsp plain flour
450ml fresh meat or
vegetable stock
2 tbsp caramelised
onion chutney

GIANT TOAD-IN-THE-HOLE

with PIBS and Super-quick Caramelised Onion Gravy

We've made this classic with two packs of pigs in blankets to generously feed a whole family. Super quick and super simple, it's the perfect midweek meal or easy alternative to a Sunday roast.

SERVES: 4
PREP TIME: 10 minutes
COOK TIME: 25 minutes

1 Preheat the oven to 220°C/200°C fan/gas mark 7.

2 Place the pigs in blankets in a large, deep roasting tin – preferably metal as this gets hotter and helps to cook the batter. Drizzle over the oil and roast in the oven for 5 minutes until the oil starts to bubble.

3 Crack the eggs into a large jug and add the flour. Whisk to form a thick paste. Slowly pour in the milk, whisking continuously until a smooth batter is formed. Add the dried herbs and season with salt and pepper.

4 Remove the hot roasting tin from the oven and carefully but quickly pour in the batter around the sausages. Return to the oven and bake for a further 20 minutes until the batter is golden and well risen.

5 In the meantime, make the gravy: place the onion and butter in a saucepan. Place over a medium heat and fry the onion for 5–8 minutes until nicely softened.

6 Sprinkle in the flour and cook for a further minute, stirring all the time to ensure it doesn't stick. Pour in the stock and gently bring to a simmer over a medium heat.

7 Stir through the chutney and season with a little salt and pepper. Gently stir the gravy as it slowly begins to thicken – this should take 3–4 minutes. Once thick and glossy, pour into a gravy boat ready to serve.

8 Remove the toad-in-the-hole from the oven and serve straight on the table alongside the onion gravy and seasonal greens.

CREAMY MUSTARD DIPPY EGGS

We've taken a traditional dippy egg and turned it on its head. Not only have we got PIB soldiers to dip in a golden runny yolk but these eggs are baked in a decadent creamy mustard and herb sauce and are made in just 20 minutes.

SERVES: 2
PREP TIME: 5 minutes
COOK TIME: 25 minutes

10 The Jolly Hog Pigs in Blankets
80ml double cream
50g thick, natural yoghurt
1 tsp Dijon mustard
1 tsp wholegrain mustard
15g fresh herbs (we like parsley and tarragon), finely chopped
sea salt and black pepper
2 medium free-range eggs
2 slices of bread, toasted, to serve

You will need 2 small, ovenproof ramekins with lids (or 2 ramekins with some kitchen foil).

1 Preheat the oven to 200°C/180°C fan/gas mark 6. Place the pigs in blankets in a roasting tin and roast in the oven for 25 minutes.

2 In the meantime, in a small jug combine the cream, yoghurt and mustards. Add the herbs to the cream. Season with salt and pepper.

3 Place the ramekins on a baking tray and divide the cream mixture between the two. In each ramekin carefully crack an egg into the centre of the mixture, leaving the yolk exposed. Put on the ramekin lids (or tightly cover with foil) and carefully place in the oven. Bake for 10–15 minutes until the white has just set but the yolk is still runny. If the egg white is still soft, return to the oven for a further 3–5 minutes.

4 Remove from the oven and serve in the ramekins alongside the cooked pigs in blankets and golden toast for dipping.

10 The Jolly Hog Pigs
   in Blankets
1kg potatoes
8 The Jolly Hog Smoked
   Rashers Streaky Bacon
2 shallots, sliced

1 garlic clove, finely
   chopped
100ml white wine
200ml double cream
sea salt and black pepper
450g reblochon, sliced

PIBS-IFLETTE

The ultimate indulgence, garlicky, cheesy potatoes topped with pigs in blankets. This recipe is great as a side to a Sunday roast or eaten straight from the tray with a spoon!

1 Preheat the oven to 180°C/160°C fan/gas mark 4.

2 Place the pigs in blankets in a roasting tin and roast in the oven for 25 minutes, then remove.

3 In the meantime, add the potatoes to a large saucepan of salted boiling water and cook for around 10 minutes or until tender. Drain and set aside to slightly cool.

4 While the potatoes are cooling, heat a frying pan over a high heat and add the bacon, shallots and garlic. Fry for 5 minutes or until the bacon starts going crispy and the shallots and garlic have softened. Pour in the white wine and continue to cook until most of the liquid has evaporated.

5 Increase the oven temperature to 200°C/180°C fan/gas mark 6.

6 Thinly slice the potatoes and layer into a baking dish along with the bacon mixture and all but four of the pigs in blankets. Pour over the double cream. Season with salt and pepper and layer the reblochon slices over the top.

7 Bake in the oven for 10–15 minutes or until the cheese is golden brown and bubbling. Once ready, top with the remaining four pigs in blankets and enjoy.

SERVES: 4
PREP TIME: 15 minutes
COOK TIME: 40 minutes

PIBS
PARCELS

It doesn't get more comforting than these bacon-wrapped stuffing balls. Perfect with your Sunday roast or Christmas dinner.

10 The Jolly Hog Caramelised Porker Sausages
1 pack of 12 Jolly Hog Smoked Rashers Streaky Bacon
2 tbsp honey
2 tbsp wholegrain mustard

1 Heat the oven to 200°C/180°C fan/gas mark 6.

2 Squeeze the meat out of the sausage skins and mash it together in a bowl. Discard the skins.

3 Roll the sausage meat into four round balls. Wrap each ball with a rasher of streaky bacon, overlapping the ends.

4 In a bowl, mix the honey and mustard together to make a glaze. Brush the parcels with the glaze.

5 Place the parcels on a baking tray and roast in the oven for 25–30 minutes until brown all over.

SERVES: 4
PREP TIME: 10 minutes
COOK TIME: 30 minutes

PIBS FESTIVE LEFTOVER TACOS

What better way to finish off your Christmas leftovers than in taco form? Load your crunchy taco shells with stuffing, pigs in blankets, sweet cranberry sauce and leftover festive cheese for a brilliant Boxing Day brunch, lunch or dinner.

SERVES: 4
PREP TIME: 20 minutes
COOK TIME: 25 minutes

10 The Jolly Hog Pigs in Blankets
12 Brussels sprouts
approx. 200g cooked stuffing
12 taco shells
12 tbsp cranberry sauce
75g Christmas cheese of your choice, grated or crumbled

1 Preheat the oven to 200°C/180°C fan/gas mark 6.

2 Place the pigs in blankets in a roasting tin and roast in the oven for 25 minutes.

3 Remove the woody base of the sprouts, then cut in half and finely shred. Place in a bowl ready for the serving board.

4 Warm the stuffing in the same oven for 10 minutes or in a microwave. Place in a bowl and add to the serving board along with the taco shells. Place the cranberry sauce in a bowl and add to the board. Add your chosen cheese.

5 Remove the pigs in blankets from the oven, place in a bowl and put on the board.

6 Take the board to the table and allow everyone to make their own tacos. Start with filling a taco shell with stuffing, followed by pigs in blankets and a spoon of cranberry sauce. Finish with a sprinkling of shredded sprouts and festive cheese.

SPRING

PIBS-TOPPED CRUMPETS

with Poached Eggs & 'Nduja Hollandaise

Whether you dip your PIBS in the runny golden yolk or let the yolk drip into the crumpet like a delicious buttery sponge, this classic brunch recipe is taken to the next level with the addition of vibrant, spicy 'nduja hollandaise.

SERVES: 2
PREP TIME: 5 minutes
COOK TIME: 25 minutes

FOR THE CRUMPETS
10 The Jolly Hog Pigs in Blankets
splash of vinegar
4 medium free-range eggs
4 crumpets, toasted
butter, to serve
sea salt and black pepper, to serve

FOR THE HOLLANDAISE
1 egg yolk
2 tsp white wine vinegar
75g salted butter, melted
1 lemon
1 heaped tsp 'nduja

1 Preheat the oven to 200°C/180°C fan/gas mark 6.

2 Place the pigs in blankets in a roasting tin and roast in the oven for 25 minutes.

3 In the meantime, make the hollandaise: place a small pan on the hob and fill 3–4cm deep with water. Place over a medium heat and allow the water to come to a gentle simmer.

4 In a heatproof dish, whisk together the egg yolk and vinegar, then place the dish on top of the saucepan ensuring it does not touch the water.

5 Slowly pour in the melted butter while continuously whisking, allowing the egg to very gently cook but not scramble. Over time, once all the butter has been added, the sauce will begin to thicken.

6 Once thick and glossy, add a squeeze of lemon followed by the 'nduja. Whisk until completely smooth, then remove from the heat and set aside.

7 Bring a pan of water with a splash of vinegar to a gentle simmer. Create a whirlpool in the water using a whisk. Carefully crack the eggs into a mug or bowl before lowering into the spinning water. Cook for 2 minutes.

8 Reduce the temperature to low and allow the eggs to finish cooking in the residual heat for approximately 4 minutes. Lift the eggs out of the water using a slotted spoon and drain on a paper towel. You may want to cook the eggs in batches.

9 To serve, butter the toasted crumpets and top each with a poached egg. Remove the pigs in blankets from the oven. Divide out on top of the poached eggs. Generously pour over the hollandaise and finish with some black pepper and a pinch of salt.

BOOOM!

33

10 The Jolly Hog Pigs
   in Blankets
4 medium free-range
   eggs
1 tbsp butter
sea salt and black pepper
2 tortilla wraps
50g feta
1 avocado, peeled, stoned
   and sliced
lime wedges, to serve

FOR THE SPICY SAUCE
6 cherry tomatoes,
   finely chopped
½ tbsp sriracha
pinch of sugar
pinch of salt

PIBS IN BREAKFAST WRAPS

with Feta, Scrambled Egg, Spicy Salsa & Avocado

Wrap up and enjoy
a PIBS brunch on the
go with these breakfast
wraps – speedy to make
and easy to eat, take
The Jolly Hog wherever
you go!

1 Preheat the oven to 200°C/180°C fan/gas mark 6.

2 Place the pigs in blankets in a roasting tin and roast in the oven for 25 minutes, then remove.

3 In the meantime, make the scrambled eggs: crack the eggs into a small pan and add the butter and seasoning. Place over a medium–low heat and slowly cook the eggs, regularly stirring to stop them from sticking. Remove from the heat while the eggs still appear slightly wet – they will continue to cook in the residual heat of the pan.

4 Place the wraps on a clean work surface and spoon on the eggs. Crumble over the feta and top with the avocado slices. Divide the sausages between the two wraps.

5 In a small bowl, combine the cherry tomatoes, sriracha, sugar and salt to make the spicy salsa. Generously spoon over before rolling, folding or placing in a bowl to serve. Wrap in kitchen foil to transport, if required.

6 Serve with some lime wedges on the side.

SERVES: 2
PREP TIME: 5 minutes
COOK TIME: 25 minutes

ULTIMATE PIBS SARNIE

Pigs in blankets with a sweet chutney is always a winning combo, but sandwiching them into a crispy baguette along with garlic mayo and crispy fried onions makes the ultimate combo.

5 The Jolly Hog Pigs in Blankets
1–2 tbsp caramelised onion chutney
1 crusty baguette, halved lengthways
5g crispy fried onions
10g rocket leaves

FOR THE GARLIC MAYO
30g mayonnaise
1 tsp garlic puree
5g fresh parsley, finely chopped

1 Preheat the oven to 200°C/180°C fan/gas mark 6.

2 Place the pigs in blankets in a roasting tin and roast in the oven for 25 minutes.

3 Spread the chutney generously on both sides of the halved baguette. Top one side with the cooked pigs in blankets.

4 To make the garlic mayo, in a bowl combine the mayonnaise, garlic puree and parsley and stir well. Drizzle over the pigs in blankets using a spoon or place in a squeezy bottle and neatly squeeze over the sausages.

5 Sprinkle over the crispy fried onions before topping with the rocket leaves. Sandwich on the lid of the baguette and then slice in half and serve.

SERVES: 1
PREP TIME: 10 minutes
COOK TIME: 25 minutes

PIBS
CARBONARA

Add a little extra porky pizzazz to this Italian classic by using pigs in blankets. A superbly scrumptious dinner in just 10 minutes.

SERVES: 2
PREP TIME: 10 minutes
COOK TIME: 10 minutes

200g dried spaghetti
½ tbsp sunflower oil
5 The Jolly Hog Pigs in Blankets, roughly chopped
1 garlic clove, finely chopped
3 egg yolks
50g Parmesan, grated, plus extra to serve
black pepper

1 Place the pasta in a pan of boiling, salted water and cook until just al dente – approximately 2 minutes short of the cook time on the packet instructions.

2 In the meantime, heat the oil in a large frying pan over a medium heat. Add the pigs in blankets to the pan. Fry for 4–5 minutes until beginning to colour before adding the garlic and frying for a further 1 minute.

3 In a separate bowl, gently whisk together the egg yolks and Parmesan and generously season with pepper.

4 Once the spaghetti is cooked al dente, drain but reserve the pasta water. Add the pasta to the frying pan and turn down the heat to low.

5 Add the egg and Parmesan mixture to the pan along with 4 generous tablespoons of the pasta water. Stir all the ingredients together and add a little more pasta water to create a creamy, glossy sauce to coat the pasta.

6 Serve the spaghetti immediately and top with more grated Parmesan and black pepper.

EGG-FRIED RICE

with PIBS

This super-speedy dish couldn't be simpler – not only that, it's also a wholesome, quick dinner, and it's all created in one pan, which saves on the washing up.

SERVES: 2*
PREP TIME: 5 minutes
COOK TIME: 10 minutes
(*or 4 as a side)

1 tbsp sesame oil
3 spring onions, chopped
1 large garlic clove, crushed
10 The Jolly Hog Pigs in Blankets, diced into small pieces
1 red pepper, deseeded and diced
100g frozen peas
250g pack pre-cooked rice
2 large free-range eggs
1 tbsp light soy sauce
1 tbsp maple syrup

1 Heat the sesame oil in a large wok over a medium–high heat. Add two-thirds of the chopped spring onion to the pan along with the garlic and pigs in blankets. Fry together for 4–5 minutes until the sausages begin to brown.

2 Add the pepper and fry for a further 2 minutes before adding the peas and rice. Stir all the ingredients together and allow the rice to warm through.

3 Make a well in the middle of the rice and crack in the eggs. Gently whisk the eggs while they cook as if you are making scrambled eggs. Break the cooked egg into large pieces, then fold through the rice mixture.

4 Finally, pour in the soy sauce and maple syrup and stir all the ingredients together. Serve the pan straight on the table and finish the dish with the remaining spring onion.

PIBS, SWEET POTATO & CHORIZO CROQUETTES

with Chilli Mayo

A cross between the traditional potato croquette and the delicious Spanish croquetas de jamón, these smoky, golden, crisp snacks are well worth the effort. Enjoy for breakfast, brunch, lunch or dinner!

MAKES: 10

PREP TIME: 15 minutes + 30 minutes freezing

COOK TIME: 1 hour 30 minutes

FOR THE CROQUETTES
2 large sweet potatoes (approx. 650g)
10 The Jolly Hog Pigs in Blankets
50g chorizo, finely diced
sea salt and black pepper
40g plain flour

FOR THE COATING
2 medium free-range eggs

50g plain flour
150g panko breadcrumbs
vegetable oil, for deep-frying

TO SERVE
100g mayonnaise
20g sriracha
squeeze of lemon juice
fresh parsley, roughly chopped

1 Preheat the oven to 200°C/180°C fan/gas mark 6.

2 Prick the sweet potatoes with a fork and bake in the oven for 1 hour on a tray.

3 About 25 minutes before the end, place the pigs in blankets in a roasting tin and roast for the remaining time. Remove from the oven and allow to cool.

4 Once the potatoes are cooked through, remove from the oven, scoop out the potato into a bowl, discarding the skins, and allow to fully cool.

5 Place the diced chorizo in a frying pan over a medium heat and fry for 3–4 minutes until just crisp and releasing its oil.

6 Stir the chorizo and cooking oil through the cooled potato and season. Sprinkle in the flour and stir to combine all the ingredients.

7 Divide the potato mixture into 10 equal balls. Take one of the cooled sausages and potato balls and wrap the potato around the sausage in a cylindrical shape, ensuring it is completely enclosed. Place on a lined baking tray and repeat with the remaining sausage and potato balls. Place the croquettes in the freezer for 30 minutes to firm up.

8 Preheat the oven to 200°C/180°C fan/gas mark 6.

42

9 In a shallow bowl, crack and lightly whisk the eggs. In another shallow bowl, add the flour, and tip the breadcrumbs into a third.

10 Take the croquettes out of the freezer and place one croquette in the egg and roll it around. Completely coat in the flour before returning to the egg bowl, coating all over again,then finally coat in the breadcrumbs. Place on the baking tray and repeat with the remaining nine croquettes.

11 Pour the oil into a heavy-bottomed saucepan, approximately 10cm deep. Heat until very hot – to test if the oil is hot, drop in a piece of stale bread. If it fiercely sizzles, the oil is ready.

12 Using a slotted spoon, gently lower two or three croquettes into the oil and fry for 3–4 minutes, occasionally turning, until they are golden all over. Drain the croquettes from the oil using the slotted spoon. Place on paper towels to remove any excess oil, then place on to a freshly lined baking tray. Repeat until all the croquettes are fried.

13 Bake in the oven for 15 minutes until golden and crisp, and warm all the way through. In a bowl stir together the mayo, sriracha and lemon juice and serve alongside the crisp croquettes. Sprinkle with fresh parsley.

43

SMOKY PIBS BREAD

An oval shaped bread boat containing The Jolly Hog Pigs in Blankets, smoky red pepper sauce, mint sauce, fresh herbs and pomegranate. Perfect for picnics, lunches and sharing.

MAKES: 4
PREP TIME: 10 minutes + 1 hour dough proving
COOK TIME: 30 minutes

FOR THE DOUGH
400g bread flour, plus extra for dusting
7g fast-action yeast
pinch of sea salt
1 tbsp sunflower oil, plus extra for greasing the bowl
235ml tepid water

FOR THE BASE SAUCE
1 tbsp rapeseed oil
1 small onion, finely chopped
100g chorizo, finely chopped
1 garlic clove, crushed
250g roasted red peppers, from a jar
75g sweet chilli sauce
10g fresh coriander, roughly chopped, plus extra to serve

FOR THE TOPPINGS
12 The Jolly Hog Pigs in Blankets
3 tbsp natural yoghurt
1 tbsp mint sauce
1 pomegranate
fresh mint, roughly chopped, to serve

You will need a stand mixer with a dough hook and a food processor.

1 First make the pizza dough: place the flour, yeast and salt in the bowl of a stand mixer and create a well in the middle. Pour in the oil and tepid water and roughly stir all the ingredients together.

2 Using the dough hook, knead the dough in the mixer on medium speed for 5–8 minutes until it is smooth and elastic. Place the dough in a lightly oiled bowl, cover with a clean tea towel and allow to rise for 1 hour.

3 In the meantime, make the base sauce. Heat the oil in a frying pan over medium–high heat and add the onion. Fry for 3–4 minutes until the onion begins to soften. Add the to the pan along with the garlic. Fry for a further 3 minutes.

4 Spoon the fried-onion mixture into a food processor and add the roasted red peppers, sweet chilli sauce and fresh coriander. Blitz to form a smooth sauce.

5 Preheat the oven to 220°C/200°C fan/gas mark 7.

6 When proved, knead the dough on a lightly floured surface for 1 minute. Divide the dough into four equal portions and roll out each ball into a 30cm-long, 15cm-wide oval and place on lightly floured baking trays.

7 Divide the sauce between each oval and spread over the dough leaving a 2cm border on each pide. Place three pigs in blankets in the middle of each bread and fold up the edges, pinching at each end to form boat-like pizzas.

8 Bake in the oven for 20 minutes until the dough is golden and risen and the pigs in blankets are cooked.

9 Combine the yoghurt and mint sauce in a small bowl and remove the seeds from the pomegranate.

10 When ready to serve, drizzle over the mint sauce and sprinkle with the pomegranate seeds. Finish with roughly chopped fresh mint and coriander.

45

PIBS & CHILLI CARAMELISED ONION-LOADED FRIES

Super-size your side of chips with the addition of sticky, spicy caramelised onions and golden melted cheese. A great sharing dish for a large gathering or family tea.

SERVES: 4–6
PREP TIME: 20 minutes
COOK TIME: 30 minutes

FOR THE FRIES
900g frozen French fries
20 The Jolly Hog Pigs in Blankets
80g grated mozzarella and Cheddar
spring onions, roughly chopped, to serve

FOR THE CHILLI CARAMELISED ONIONS
40g salted butter
2 red onions, thinly sliced
1 tbsp fresh thyme leaves
½–1 tbsp chilli flakes, depending on heat
2 tbsp balsamic vinegar
2 tbsp water
60g soft brown sugar

1 Preheat the oven to 200°C/180°C fan/gas mark 6.

2 Place the fries and pigs in blankets in a large roasting tin and roast in the oven for 25 minutes.

3 In the meantime, make the caramelised onions: melt the butter in a heavy-bottomed saucepan over a medium heat and add the onions and thyme leaves. Gently fry for 5–6 minutes until the onions begin to soften, then sprinkle in the chilli flakes.

4 Pour in the balsamic vinegar along with the water and sprinkle in the sugar. Stir all the ingredients together and bring to a simmer. Allow to gently simmer and reduce for approximately 10–15 minutes.

5 Once the onions are reduced and sticky, set aside. Remove the chips and sausages from the oven and place in a heatproof dish. Heat the grill to medium–high.

6 Spoon over the caramelised onions and sprinkle over the cheese. Place under the grill for 3–4 minutes until the cheese has melted and is bubbling.

7 Serve on the table with a sprinkling of spring onions and eat straight away.

1 tbsp salted butter
1 onion, chopped
1 garlic clove, crushed
sea salt
1 tbsp dried oregano
10 The Jolly Hog Pigs
   in Blankets, chopped
   into 3 pieces
200g mixed mushrooms,
   roughly chopped
100g kale, roughly
   chopped
1 heaped tbsp plain flour

1 tbsp bouillon powder,
   or 1 vegetable stock
   cube
500ml freshly boiled
   hot water
250ml double cream
500g fresh gnocchi
50g Gruyère, grated

TO SERVE
fresh green salad
bread

CREAMY
BAKED PIBS
& GNOCCHI

with Mushroom & Kale

This baked gnocchi is all
levels of autumn comfort
– a great family dish that
will fill tummies and
souls alike.

SERVES: 4
PREP TIME: 10 minutes
COOK TIME: 35 minutes

1 Preheat the oven to 200°C/180°C fan/gas mark 6.

2 Melt the butter in a large frying pan over a
medium heat. Add the onion and fry for 3–4 minutes
until it begins to soften. Add the garlic along with
a pinch of salt and fry for a further 2 minutes.

3 Sprinkle in the oregano and add the pigs in
blankets to the pan. Fry the sausages for 3–4 minutes
until they start to colour. Add the mushrooms and
kale to the pan and fry for another 3–4 minutes
until the kale begins to wilt.

4 Sprinkle in the flour and stir through the pan.
Dissolve the bouillon powder in the hot water
and slowly add to the pan. As the sauce begins to
thicken, add the rest of the stock before pouring
in the cream.

5 Stir the gnocchi into the sauce and then remove
from the heat. Spoon into an ovenproof dish,
sprinkle the grated Gruyère over the top and bake
in the oven for 20 minutes until the top is golden
and bubbling.

6 Remove from the oven and serve alongside a fresh
green salad and bread for dipping.

PIBS & MEXICAN RICE-STUFFED PEPPERS

with Smoked Cheese & Soured Cream Dressing

Serve just half a pepper with salad for a light bite, or two halves for a more substantial dinner. Try making the Mexican rice in advance and you'll be able to whip up this dish in next to no time.

MAKES: 8
PREP TIME: 25 minutes
COOK TIME: 45 minutes

FOR THE MEXICAN RICE

200g brown rice
1 tbsp vegetable bouillon
600ml water
10 The Jolly Hog Pigs in Blankets
½ tbsp sunflower oil
1 onion, finely diced
1 garlic clove, crushed
sea salt
2 heaped tsp chipotle paste
1 tsp smoked sweet paprika
½ tsp ground coriander
½ tsp ground cumin
15g fresh coriander, finely chopped

FOR THE PEPPERS

4 peppers, mixture of colours, halved and deseeded
50g smoked Cheddar, grated

FOR THE SOURED CREAM DRESSING

2 tbsp soured cream
1 tbsp mayo
½ tbsp garlic puree
sea salt and black pepper

TO SERVE

fresh green salad or Mexican nachos, to serve

---

1 Preheat the oven to 200°C/180°C fan/gas mark 6.

2 Rinse the rice and place in a large saucepan along with the bouillon and water. Bring to the boil, lower the heat and allow to gently simmer for 25 minutes until cooked. Add more water if required.

3 In the meantime, place the pigs in blankets in a roasting tin and roast in the oven for 20 minutes. Remove from the oven.

4 Heat the oil in a frying pan and add the onion. Fry over a medium heat for 4–5 minutes until the onion starts to soften. Add the garlic along with a pinch of salt and fry for a further 2 minutes.

5 Add the chipotle paste along with the paprika, ground coriander and cumin and mix to a thick paste. Gently fry for 1 minute, stirring continuously to ensure it does not stick.

6 Remove the paste from the heat and add the drained cooked rice. Stir all the ingredients together and sprinkle in two-thirds of the fresh coriander.

50

7 Take the pigs in blankets out of the oven, dice them up into small pieces, then stir through the rice.

8 Spoon the rice mixture into each pepper half and place on a baking tray. Sprinkle over the cheese and bake in the oven for 18–20 minutes until the cheese is crisp and golden and the peppers are tender.

9 To make the dressing, simply combine the soured cream, mayo, garlic puree and seasoning in a bowl – set aside until ready to serve.

10 Place the peppers on a serving plate and drizzle over the dressing. Finish with the remaining fresh coriander and serve alongside a fresh green salad or nachos.

HARISSA-ROASTED PIBS & VEGGIES

with Hasselback Potatoes & Chermoula

Vibrant in colour and flavour. Try your hand at this awesome traybake packed full of spices.

SERVES: 4
PREP TIME: 10 minutes
COOK TIME: 45 minutes

FOR THE HASSELBACK POTATOES
500g new potatoes
1 tbsp rapeseed oil
1 tbsp smoked paprika
sea salt

FOR THE HARISSA MARINADE
40g harissa paste
30g maple syrup
squeeze of lemon juice

FOR THE ROASTED VEGGIES
200g mixed mini peppers
1 courgette, cut into thick chunks
1 red onion, cut into wedges
10 The Jolly Hog Pigs in Blankets
100g sliced kale

FOR THE CHERMOULA
30g fresh coriander
30g fresh parsley
2 preserved lemons, or 2 tbsp lemon juice
1 tsp coriander seeds, toasted
1 tsp ground cumin
3 tbsp rapeseed oil
1–2 tbsp water
sea salt

You will need a food processor.

1 Preheat the oven to 200°C/180°C fan/gas mark 6.

2 Thinly slice the potatoes with a sharp knife without going all the way through. Place the potatoes in a large roasting tin, sprinkle with the oil and paprika and season with salt. Roast for 20 minutes.

3 In the meantime, make the harissa marinade. In a small bowl, whisk together the harissa paste, maple syrup and a squeeze of lemon juice. Loosen further with a dash of water, if required.

4 When the potatoes have roasted for 20 minutes, remove from the oven and turn them. Add the mini peppers, courgette and onion wedges to the pan along with the pigs in blankets. Pour in the marinade and stir all the ingredients to coat. Return the roasting tin to the oven for a further 20 minutes.

5 Finally, add the kale to the roasting tin and cook for 5 minutes more.

6 Before serving, make the chermoula. Place the coriander, parsley, preserved lemons or lemon juice, coriander seeds and ground cumin. Pour in the oil along with the water. Blitz until combined and then season to taste.

7 Serve the roasting tin straight on the table. Generously drizzle the veggies and sausages with some of the chermoula and serve the remaining sauce in a bowl on the side.

53

PIBS & PINEAPPLE BBQ SKEWERS

Grilled pineapple, zesty lime and sweet chilli just sing of the bright and sunny flavours of the Caribbean. Try these easy skewers when you next fire up the barbie, or bring the sunshine indoors and simply cook them under the grill.

MAKES: 2 large skewers
PREP TIME: 5 minutes
COOK TIME: 10 minutes

10 The Jolly Hog Pigs in Blankets
3 spring onions, each trimmed and cut into three
8 large pineapple wedges
4 tbsp sweet chilli sauce, plus extra to serve
1 limes, to serve

You will need 2 long metal skewers.

1 Preheat the grill or barbecue to medium–high heat.

2 Thread a pig in blanket onto a skewer followed by a piece of spring onion and a pineapple wedge. Repeat this pattern another three times so there are four of each ingredient on the skewer, then finish with a final pig in blanket. Repeat with the second skewer.

3 Drizzle 1 tablespoon of the chilli sauce onto one side of each skewer. If cooking under the grill, place the skewers sauce-side up; if cooking on a barbecue, place them sauce-side down.

4 Grill the skewers for 3–4 minutes until the sausage is cooked on one side and the pineapple and spring onion are beginning to char.

5 Flip the skewers and drizzle over the remaining 2 tablespoons of chilli sauce. Place back under the grill on or the barbecue and grill on the other side for a further 3–4 minutes.

6 Place the skewers on a large serving board or plate. Finely grate over the zest of one of the limes. Slice the second lime into wedges and serve alongside the skewers with a bowl of sweet chilli sauce for extra dipping.

PIBS SUSHI

Our take on a DIY pig in blanket, these PIBS sushi rolls are perfect as a party canapé and are sure to impress.

SERVES: 2
PREP TIME: 10 minutes
+ 30 minutes chilling
COOK TIME: 20 minutes

100g carrot, peeled and cut into matchsticks
100g parsnip, peeled and cut into matchsticks
Sunflower oil, for drizzling and deep-frying
4 The Jolly Hog Smoked Rashers Streaky Bacon
6 The Jolly Hog Proper Porker Sausages
1 medium egg
10g plain flour
10g panko breadcrumbs
10g sriracha mayo
a sprinkle of black seeds

1 Preheat the oven to 170°C/150°C fan/gas mark 3.

2 Put the vegetable sticks in a baking dish and drizzle with the oil. Roast them in the oven for 8 minutes. Remove and leave to cool.

3 When the sticks are cool, put three of them together and wrap them in a slice of streaky bacon, repeat until you have used all the bacon.

4 Squeeze the sausage meat out of the cases. Lay a large piece of cling film in front of you. Place the sausage meat on the cling film and spread it into a thin layer of meat. Put the wrapped vegetables on the meat in a line and roll it up into a cylinder shape using the cling film to help you.

5 Beat the egg in a shallow plate. Put the flour and breadcrumbs on two separate plates. Roll the 'sushi' in the flour, then the beaten egg and finally the breadcrumbs. Wrap in cling film, tighten the ends to secure and chill the roll in the fridge for 30 minutes.

6 Heat the oil in a deep frying pan over a medium–high heat and deep-fry the roll at 160°C for 8 minutes. When it is done, drain on paper towels, slice, then drizzle the sriracha mayo on top and sprinkle with the black seeds.

SUMMER

SPICY CHIPOTLE SKEWERS

These spicy Mexican-inspired skewers are not for the fainthearted. With lashings of chipotle paste, these summer skewers are served with a creamy avocado mayo for a cool kick.

MAKES: 3 large skewers
PREP TIME: 5 minutes
COOK TIME: 10 minutes

FOR THE SKEWERS
9 The Jolly Hog Pigs in Blankets (1 for the chef!)
1 red pepper, deseeded and cut into 9 chunky pieces
1 yellow pepper, deseeded and cut into 9 chunky pieces
1 courgette, trimmed and cut into 9 thick slices
9 baby corn
fresh coriander, chopped, to serve

FOR THE MARINADE
40g chipotle paste
40g runny honey
zest and juice of 1 lime

FOR THE AVOCADO MAYO
1 ripe avocado
40g mayonnaise
juice of ½ lime
sea salt and black pepper

You will need 3 long, metal skewers and a blender or food processor.

1 Preheat the grill or barbecue to medium–high.

2 Thread a pig in blanket onto a skewer, followed by a piece of each veg. Repeat so there are three of each ingredient. Repeat on the remaining two skewers.

3 To make the marinade, in a bowl stir together the chipotle paste, honey, lime zest and juice.

4 Brush half the marinade on one side of each skewer. Place under the grill, marinade-side up, or if cooking on the barbecue, place marinade-side down.

5 Cook for 3–4 minutes until one side of the sausages is cooked and the vegetables are beginning to char. Remove and brush the other side with the remaining marinade. Cook for a further 3–4 minutes.

6 Meanwhile, make the avocado mayo: cut the avocado in half, scoop out the flesh and discard the skin and stone. Place the flesh in a blender or food processor, with the mayonnaise, lime juice and a little salt and pepper. Blend to smooth sauce. Transfer to a bowl.

7 Remove the skewers from the heat and place on a serving board with the avocado mayo for dipping. Serve sprinkled with coriander.

FOR THE FRITTATA

1 tbsp rapeseed oil
10 The Jolly Hog Pigs
  in Blankets
250g new potatoes,
  cooked and sliced
100g mixed cherry
  tomatoes, half cut
  in half
100g baby spinach
8 medium free-range
  eggs
sea salt and black pepper

½ tbsp smoked paprika
½ tbsp dried mixed
  herbs
30g mature Cheddar,
  grated

**FOR THE SOURED CREAM AND
CHIVE DIP**

2 tbsp soured cream
1 tbsp mayonnaise
1 tsp garlic puree
10g chives, finely
  chopped

PIBS
BREAKFAST FRITTATA & SOURED CREAM & CHIVE DIP

1 Preheat the grill to high.

2 Heat the oil in a deep, ovenproof frying pan over a medium heat and add the pigs in blankets. Fry the sausages for 4–5 minutes until they start to brown.

3 Add the cooked potatoes to the pan and continue to fry for a further 3–4 minutes until the potato begins to colour.

4 Add all the tomatoes to the pan along with the spinach. Fry until the spinach leaves have wilted.

5 In a large jug whisk the eggs with salt, pepper, paprika and mixed herbs. Whisk until all the ingredients are combined, then pour the egg mixture into the pan. Allow to gently cook on the hob for 2–3 minutes until you can start to see the frittata firm up – it will still appear runny on the top.

6 Remove the pan from the heat. Sprinkle the frittata with the grated cheese and place under the grill for 4–5 minutes until golden and bubbling.

7 Remove the pan from the grill and allow the frittata to sit for 2 minutes to slightly firm up while you make the soured cream dip. Combine all the ingredients for the dip in a bowl and season to taste.

8 Slice the frittata into quarters and serve alongside the dip.

A brunch for a crowd in just 15 minutes, this frittata has everything you need for brekkie and more. Also great as a speedy midweek meal or al fresco lunch.

SERVES: 4–6
PREP TIME: 5 minutes
COOK TIME: 20 minutes

61

TERIYAKI-GLAZED PIBS IN LETTUCE CUPS

with Fresh, Crunchy Matchstick Veg

Create these fresh, fun, flavour-filled mouthfuls in no time at all for a speedy midweek meal or for a pretty party platter.

MAKES: 5 cups
PREP TIME: 5 minutes
COOK TIME: 35 minutes

FOR THE TERIYAKI GLAZE
200ml water
50g soft brown sugar
30ml light soy sauce
1 tsp garlic puree
½ tbsp rice wine vinegar
1 tsp cornflour
thumb-sized piece of fresh ginger, peeled and finely grated

FOR THE LETTUCE CUPS
10 The Jolly Hog Pigs in Blankets

1 carrot, peeled
¼ cucumber
5 radishes
5 lettuce leaves

TO SERVE
30g cashews, toasted and roughly chopped
handful of fresh mint leaves, roughly chopped
chilli flakes (optional)
lime wedges

1 Preheat the oven to 200°C/180°C fan/gas mark 6.

2 First, make the teriyaki glaze: place all the glaze ingredients in a heavy-bottomed saucepan over a medium heat and whisk together. Once all the ingredients have combined well, heat to a simmer and reduce for 5–8 minutes until glossy and thick, regularly stirring. Remove from the heat and allow to slightly cool.

3 Place the pigs in blankets in a roasting tin and spoon over a tablespoon of the teriyaki glaze to coat. Roast in the oven for 15 minutes.

4 Remove the sausages from the oven, turn over and spoon over a little more sauce. Return to the oven for another 10 minutes.

5 In the meantime, prepare the vegetables. Slice the carrot and cucumber into matchsticks and set aside. Thinly slice the radishes.

6 When the sausages are cooked, remove from the oven and place two in each lettuce cup. Top with the matchstick vegetables and radish slices. Spoon over a little more teriyaki sauce, if desired, and place on a serving plate.

7 Sprinkle the chopped cashews, mint and chilli flakes, if using, on top and serve with lime wedges.

ROASTED GARLIC SPREAD, PIBS & TOMATO BRUSCHETTA

with Balsamic Glaze & Basil

For a light bite, simple snack or chunky canapé, these PIBS on bruschetta pack a flavour punch with a sweet, roasted garlic spread, zingy tomato and fresh basil.

FOR THE GARLIC SPREAD
1 large garlic bulb
1 tbsp rapeseed oil
sea salt and black pepper
3 tbsp crème fraîche

FOR THE BRUSCHETTA
10 The Jolly Hog Pigs in Blankets
1 large baguette
10 cherry tomatoes, halved
1 tbsp balsamic glaze
black pepper
10 fresh basil leaves

1 Preheat the oven to 200°C/180°C fan/gas mark 6.

2 Slice the top off the garlic bulb to just expose the cloves. Drizzle over the oil, season with salt and pepper, place in some kitchen foil and tightly wrap. Roast in the oven on a tray for 30 minutes until the garlic is very soft.

3 Remove from the oven and leave to completely cool. Squeeze the softened garlic into a bowl and stir through the crème fraîche to create a smooth paste. Season generously with salt and pepper and set aside.

4 Place the pigs in blankets in a roasting tin and roast in the oven for 25 minutes.

5 Slice the baguette on the diagonal into 10 thick slices. Place in the toaster or under a hot grill until golden.

6 When ready to assemble, top the toasted slices generously with the garlic spread. Add the cooked pigs in blankets and tomato halves. Drizzle over the balsamic glaze and finish with a crack of black pepper and the basil leaves.

MAKES: 10
PREP TIME: 10 minutes
COOK TIME: 55 minutes

PIBS
SKEWER
MARINADES

Try these easy marinades to pimp up your PIBs.

SERVES: 2
PREP TIME: 5 minutes
COOK TIME: 10 minutes

You will need an extra-long metal skewer.

SWEET CHILLI, LIME & SESAME

10 The Jolly Hog Pigs in Blankets
1 tbsp sweet chilli sauce
½ tbsp honey
1 lime, halved
½ tbsp sesame seeds
1 tsp chilli flakes (optional)

1 Preheat the grill to high.

2 Thread the pigs in blankets onto the skewer and place on a baking tray.

3 In a bowl combine the sweet chilli and honey and squeeze in the juice of half the lime. Brush half of the marinade over the skewers and place under the grill, marinade-side up, for 3–4 minutes.

4 Remove the skewer from the grill, flip and brush the other side of the sausages with the remaining marinade. Place back under the grill for 3–4 minutes.

5 Once cooked, remove from the grill. Place the skewer on a serving dish and sprinkle over the sesame seeds and chilli flakes, if using. Finish with a grating of lime zest and serve with lime wedges.

MUSTARD, MAPLE & ORANGE

10 The Jolly Hog Pigs in Blankets
½ tbsp Dijon mustard
½ wholegrain mustard
1 tbsp maple syrup
zest of 1 orange

1 Preheat the grill to high.

2 Thread the pigs in blankets onto the skewer and place on a baking tray.

3 In a bowl combine the mustards and maple syrup, then brush half over the sausages. Place the sausages under the grill, mustard-side up, for 3–4 minutes.

4 Remove the skewer from the grill, flip and brush the other side of the sausages with the remaining marinade. Place back under the grill for 3–4 minutes.

5 Once cooked, remove from the grill. Place the skewer on a serving dish and scatter with the orange zest.

HONEY & SOY GLAZED PIBS POKE BOWL

with Spicy Satay Sauce

Fresh, vibrant and spicy flavours, this poke bowl is a ray of sunshine regardless of the weather outside!

SERVES: 2
PREP TIME: 5 minutes
COOK TIME: 25 minutes

FOR THE GLAZED SAUSAGES
8 The Jolly Hog Pigs in Blankets
30g runny honey
15ml soy sauce
thumb-sized piece of fresh ginger, peeled and finely grated

FOR THE SATAY SAUCE
50g good-quality smooth peanut butter
10g runny honey
½ tbsp soy sauce
juice of ½ lime
1 tbsp sriracha
2 tbsp ice-cold water

FOR THE POKE BOWL
400g cooked sticky or sushi rice
1 carrot, cut into thin matchsticks
½ cucumber, peeled into ribbons with a vegetable peeler
4 radishes, sliced into strips
1 pepper, sliced into strips
100g cooked edamame beans
40g cashews, toasted and roughly chopped
4 lime wedges

1 Preheat the oven to 200°C/180°C fan/gas mark 6.

2 Place the pigs in blankets in a roasting tin and roast in the oven for 15 minutes.

3 In the meantime, make the glaze by combining the honey, soy sauce and ginger in a bowl.

4 Remove the pigs in blankets from the oven, drizzle over the glaze and return to the oven for a further 10 minutes until sticky and caramelised.

5 To make the satay sauce, put the peanut butter, honey and soy sauce in a bowl, then squeeze in the lime juice. Add the sriracha along with the water and whisk all the ingredients together to form a thick, glossy sauce.

6 When ready to assemble, spoon the sticky rice into two serving bowls. Divide the carrot, then the cucumber between the two bowls. Add the radishes and pepper and scatter in the edamame beans.

7 Remove the glazed sausages from the oven, add to the rice bowls and drizzle over the satay sauce. Sprinkle the cashews over the bowls and serve each with lime wedges.

10 The Jolly Hog Pigs in Blankets

1 tbsp salted butter

250g leek, finely sliced

1 large garlic clove, crushed

sea salt and black pepper

120g courgette, grated

15g coriander, stems finely diced and leaves roughly chopped

15g parsley, stems finely diced and leaves roughly chopped

150g baby spinach

1 tbsp good-quality pesto

4 medium free-range eggs

50g feta

FOR THE HARISSA YOGHURT

1 heaped tsp harissa paste

2 tbsp natural yoghurt

squeeze of lemon juice

You will need a large, deep frying pan with a lid.

GREEN
SHAKSHUKA

with Crumbled Feta & Harissa Yoghurt

A take on the traditional tomato-based shakshuka, this bright and bold brunch dish is packed full of iron-rich green veggies but still feels like a real treat.

1 Preheat the oven to 200°C/180°C fan/gas mark 6. Place the pigs in blankets in a roasting tin and roast in the oven for 25 minutes.

2 In the meantime, melt the butter in a large frying pan over a medium heat. Add the leek and gently fry for 4–5 minutes until they begin to soften. Add the garlic and a generous pinch of salt and pepper and fry for a further 2–3 minutes.

3 Add the grated courgette and coriander and parsley stems. Fry for 3 minutes and then add the spinach leaves. Allow the spinach to gently wilt, then stir through the pesto and cooked sausages.

4 Make four wells in the leek and courgette mixture and crack an egg into each hole. Turn down the heat to low and cover with the lid. Allow the eggs to gently poach for 5–7 minutes until the whites have just cooked but the yolks are still runny.

5 In a small bowl combine the harissa paste, yoghurt and squeeze of lemon juice.

6 Remove the pan from the heat, take off the lid and crumble over the feta. Finish by sprinkling over the coriander and parsley leaves. Serve the pan on the table alongside the harissa yoghurt.

SERVES: 4

PREP TIME: 5 minutes

COOK TIME: 35 minutes

SHARING CAESAR SALAD

with PIBS

Switching the classic chicken for little pigs in blankets is a surprisingly perfect swap – with their salty bacon blankets and herby sausage centres, our pigs in blankets work perfectly with the traditional flavours of Caesar salad for a super summer spread.

SERVES: 4
PREP TIME: 10 minutes
COOK TIME: 25 minutes

10 The Jolly Hog Pigs in Blankets
2 slices of sourdough bread, torn or cut into cubes
½ tbsp sunflower oil

FOR THE CAESAR SAUCE
65g mayonnaise
4 anchovy fillets, very finely chopped
10g Parmesan, finely grated, plus extra, shaved, to serve
½ tsp Dijon mustard
2 tbsp lemon juice
1–2 tbsp ice-cold water

TO SERVE
2 cos lettuce hearts
2 medium hard-boiled free-range eggs, sliced into quarters
black pepper

1 Preheat the oven to 200°C/180°C fan/gas mark 6.

2 Place the pigs in blankets in a roasting tin and roast in the oven for 25 minutes.

3 Place the sourdough slices in a bowl. Sprinkle with the oil and toss to fully coat. Add to the roasting tin for the final 5 minutes of cooking until toasted and golden.

4 In the meantime, make the Caesar sauce. Spoon the mayonnaise into a bowl and add the anchovies, grated Parmesan and Dijon mustard. Pour in the lemon juice and whisk together. Add the water to loosen if required. Set aside until ready to serve.

5 When ready to serve, shred the lettuce and place on a large serving plate or bowl. Scatter over the cooked pigs in blankets and toasted sourdough pieces. Generously drizzle over the prepared sauce and finish the dish with hard-boiled eggs, extra Parmesan shavings and a crack of black pepper.

FOR THE BATTERED PIBS
200ml beer or lager
125g self-raising flour
pinch of sea salt
10 The Jolly Hog Pigs
   in Blankets

FOR THE CHIPS
400g potatoes
75ml sunflower oil
sea salt and black pepper

TO SERVE
curry sauce
mushy peas

BATTERED
PIBS

with Salt
& Pepper Chips

A classic British dish but in miniature form. Why not recreate these chip-shop staples at home for your Friday night 'fake-away'?

1 Preheat the oven to 220°C/200°C fan/gas mark 7.

2 First, make the batter: pour the beer into a large jug and whisk in the flour to form a silky batter. Season with a little salt and allow to sit for 10 minutes.

3 Leaving the skins on, slice the potatoes into 1cm wide chips and, using paper towels, dab off any excess moisture.

4 Put the chips into a large roasting tin and generously drizzle with the oil and sprinkle with sea salt and black pepper. Roast in the oven, turning twice, for 20–25 minutes until golden and crisp.

5 In the meantime make your battered sausages: heat the rest of the sunflower oil over a medium-high heat until very hot.

6 Whisk the rested batter to remove any lumps. Working in batches, dip the sausages in the batter, ensuring they are fully coated before carefully placing in the hot oil. Fry for 5–6 minutes until the batter is golden and crisp and the sausages are cooked through. Place on paper towels to remove any excess oil and repeat until all the sausages are cooked.

7 Serve the battered sausages on top of the chips straight from the oven alongside the warmed curry sauce and mushy peas.

SERVES: 2
PREP TIME: 10 minutes
+ 10 minutes resting
COOK TIME: 25 minutes

73

375g block puff pastry
20 The Jolly Hog Pigs
   in Blankets
10 tsp fruit chutney
   (we use fig)
1 egg, gently beaten
2 tbsp nigella seeds

FOR THE MUSTARD MAYO
2 tbsp mayonnaise
½ tbsp wholegrain
   mustard

1 Preheat the oven to 200°C/180°C fan/gas mark 6.
Line a baking tray with greaseproof paper.

2 Roll out the puff pastry on a clean surface and
using a knife divide it into 20 rectangles.

3 Spoon ½ teaspoon of the chutney on each piece
of pastry, then place a pig in blanket on top.

4 Roll up the pastry around the sausage and secure
on the bottom by gently pinching together the
pastry. Place crease-side down on the lined
baking tray.

5 Using a pastry brush, brush the rolls with a little
of the whisked egg. Using a sharp knife score the
top of each roll twice. Sprinkle each sausage roll
with the nigella seeds and then bake in the oven for
25 minutes until golden brown and nicely puffed up.

6 While the rolls are baking, make the mustard mayo
by combining the mayonnaise and mustard in a bowl.

7 Serve the sausage rolls hot from the oven with
the mustard mayo or allow to cool and eat cold.

PIBS & FRUIT CHUTNEY SAUSAGE ROLLS

with Mustard Mayo Dipping Sauce

Whether you are in
need of a party nibble
or an on-the-go snack
for a park picnic, you
can't go wrong with a
sausage roll! Try these
mini PIB sausage rolls
with a sweet twist of fruit
chutney and a mustard
mayo for those adult
dippers!

MAKES: 20
PREP TIME: 10 minutes
COOK TIME: 25 minutes

PIBS
COCKTAIL

with Homemade Thousand Island Sauce

A piggy new take on a culinary classic, why not try making pigs-in-blankets cocktail with a punchy thousand island sauce served on crunchy lettuce wedges and creamy avocado. Perfect for a light lunch or dinner party starter.

SERVES: 4
PREP TIME: 5 minutes
COOK TIME: 25 minutes

12 The Jolly Hog Pigs in Blankets
1 large cos lettuce heart
1 avocado
smoked paprika, to serve

FOR THE SAUCE
30g burger sauce or sweet pickle relish

25g pickled gherkins, finely chopped
100g mayonnaise
30g tomato ketchup
black pepper

You will need 4 stemmed serving glasses.

1 Preheat the oven to 200°C/180°C fan/gas mark 6.

2 Place the pigs in blankets in a roasting tin and roast in the oven for 25 minutes.

3 In the meantime, make the thousand island sauce: place the burger sauce or sweet pickle relish, chopped gherkins, mayonnaise and ketchup in a bowl and stir to combine. Season with a little black pepper. Set aside until ready to serve.

4 Finely shred the lettuce and place a little in the bottom of each serving glass. Slice the avocado in half, remove and discard the stone and carefully scoop out the flesh. Thinly slice and place a couple of slices in each glass.

5 Top the lettuce and avocado with three pigs in blankets per glass before generously spooning over the prepared sauce. Finish each dish with a small sprinkling of paprika and serve.

MINI PIBS
SPICY FAJITAS

A classic family recipe for all to enjoy. Try our porky twist on the perfect midweek meal, made in a flash.

SERVES: 4
PREP TIME: 5 minutes
COOK TIME: 15 minutes

1 tbsp sunflower oil
1 red onion, thinly sliced
10 The Jolly Hog Pigs in Blankets, chopped into 3 pieces
2 carrots, thinly sliced into strips
1 red pepper, deseeded and thinly sliced into strips
10g fresh coriander, roughly chopped

FOR THE FAJITA SAUCE
25g sriracha
½ tbsp garlic puree
25g sweet chilli sauce

1 tbsp sweet smoked paprika
1 tsp ground cinnamon
1 tsp ground cumin
squeeze of lime juice
2 tbsp water
pinch of sea salt

TO SERVE
12–16 mini tortilla wraps
1 tub of guacamole
1 tub of tomato salsa
pot of soured cream
small lettuce, shredded
200g grated Cheddar
8 lime wedges

1 Heat the oil in a large frying pan and add the onion. Fry for 2–3 minutes over a medium heat until the onion begins to soften.

2 Add the pigs in blankets to the onion. Fry for 2–3 minutes before adding the carrots and pepper. Fry for a further 4 minutes until the carrot begins to soften.

3 In a bowl stir together the sriracha, garlic puree and sweet chilli sauce. Sprinkle in the paprika, cinnamon and cumin before adding a squeeze of lime, the water and a pinch of salt. Stir all the ingredients together.

4 Add the fajita sauce to the pan and lower the heat. Allow the vegetables and sausages to gently simmer in the sauce for 5–6 minutes until the ingredients have cooked and the sauce has thickened.

5 Remove from the heat and stir through the fresh coriander. Serve on the table alongside the wraps. Serve the guacamole, salsa, soured cream, lettuce and Cheddar in individual bowls and finish with lime wedges.

PIBS, APPLE & LEEK PASTIES

Pack for a picnic or enjoy warm straight from the oven for dinner, these pasties are a real crowd-pleaser and perfect for filling up the freezer – you can thank yourself later!

MAKES: 6
PREP TIME: 20 minutes*, plus 15 minutes chilling
COOK TIME: 45 minutes

FOR THE PASTRY
225g salted butter, fridge-cold and cut into cubes
450g plain flour
250ml water

FOR THE FILLING
250g peeled potato, cut into 1cm cubes
1 tbsp butter
200g leek

10 The Jolly Hog Pigs in Blankets, diced into small pieces
1 garlic clove, crushed
1 tbsp dried mixed herbs
100g apple, grated
sea salt and black pepper
1 egg

1 First, make the pastry: place the cold butter into a food processor and then add the flour. Briefly pulse to form a sandy, breadcrumb-like texture, then add the water.

2 Blitz until the mixture just starts to come together, then turn out on to a clean worksurface. Briefly knead until a smooth dough is formed, then wrap in cling film and chill in the fridge for 15 minutes.

3 In the meantime, place the potato cubes in a pan of salted water, bring to the boil, then simmer for 5–8 minutes until the potato cubes are tender but still holding form. Drain and allow to cool.

4 In a frying pan melt the butter, then add the leek and fry for 2–3 minutes. Add the pigs in blankets to the leek pan. Fry for a further 5 minutes until the sausages begin to cook.

5 Add the garlic and mixed herbs to the pan and fry for a further 2 minutes. Remove from the heat, spoon into a large mixing bowl and allow to cool.

6 Once cooled, add the grated apple to the mixing bowl along with the cooled potato cubes. Gently mix everything together and season with a little salt and pepper.

7 Preheat the oven to 200°C/180°C fan/gas mark 6. Line a large baking tray with baking paper and remove the pastry from the fridge.

8 Divide the pastry into six equal portions and roll into approximately 20cm-diameter circles – use an upturned side plate and knife to create perfect circles, if desired.

9 Divide the sausage, leek and potato mixture between each pastry circle, placing the mixture on one half so you can fold the other half of the pastry over.

10 Lightly whisk the egg in a bowl, and using a pastry brush, brush a little egg around the edge of each pastry circle. Fold over the pastry to form a semi-circle and gently press the pastry edges together to enclose the filling.

11 Use a traditional pasty crimping technique or simply pinch the pastry edge together between your thumb and index finger. Brush the pasties with a little more egg. Transfer to the lined baking tray and bake for 25 minutes until the pastry is golden and crisp.

12 Serve warm straight from the oven or allow to cool and eat cold on the go.

PIBS &
MAPLE SYRUP-
TOPPED FRENCH TOAST

A take on the bacon and maple classic. We've ramped it up another level with the addition of our perfectly porky pigs in blankets. Make this recipe extra special by using brioche.

SERVES: 2
PREP TIME: 5 minutes
COOK TIME: 20 minutes

10 The Jolly Hog Pigs in Blankets
1 free-range egg
60ml milk
20ml double cream
1 tsp soft brown sugar
2 thick slices of white bread or brioche
1 tbsp salted butter

4 tbsp maple syrup, to serve

1 Preheat the oven to 200°C/180°C fan/gas mark 6.

2 Place the pigs in blankets in a roasting tin and roast in the oven for 20 minutes.

3 In the meantime, make the French toast. In a shallow bowl crack in the egg and pour in the milk and cream. Sprinkle in the sugar and lightly whisk to combine.

4 Lie the slices of bread in the egg mixture and allow them to absorb it, turning the slices to ensure both sides are soaked.

5 Melt the butter in a large frying pan over a medium heat. Lay the soaked bread in the hot butter and fry for 2–3 minutes until golden and crispy, then carefully flip and cook on the second side for 2–3 minutes.

6 Once golden, remove from the pan, place on a chopping board and slice in half. Place the French toast onto serving plates and top with the cooked pigs in blankets. Pour over the maple syrup and serve immediately.

LOADED HASH BROWNS

with Homemade Smoky Beans & Cheese

The combination of hash browns, bacon and sausages can only be made better by the addition of smoky homemade beans and melted cheese. A great alternative to a weekend fry-up.

SERVES: 4
PREP TIME: 5 minutes
COOK TIME: 30 minutes

FOR THE LOADED HASH BROWNS
10 The Jolly Hog Pigs in Blankets
12 frozen hash browns
1 tbsp smoked rapeseed oil
80g smoked Cheddar, grated

FOR THE SMOKY BEANS
1 small red onion, finely sliced
1 tbsp smoked rapeseed oil
sea salt
½ tbsp garlic puree
1 tbsp good-quality smoked paprika
1 tbsp sun-dried tomato paste
1 tbsp maple syrup
2 x 400g tins cannellini beans
150ml good-quality passata
40ml water

1 Preheat the oven to 200°C/180°C fan/gas mark 6.

2 Place the pigs in blankets and hash browns in a large roasting tin and roast in the oven for 25 minutes.

3 Place the sliced onion in a saucepan with the smoked oil. Fry over a low–medium heat for 5–8 minutes until the onion is soft. Add a generous pinch of salt and then add the garlic puree. Fry for a further 1 minute.

4 Add the paprika, tomato paste and maple syrup to the pan and stir to combine. Tip in the beans, passata and water, turn up the heat to medium and then bring to a simmer. Gently simmer for approximately 8–10 minutes until the sauce has reduced to a thick consistency. Season again if necessary.

5 Remove the hash browns and sausages from the oven and heat the grill to medium–high.

6 Pour the smoky beans over the hash browns and sausages and sprinkle with the grated cheese. Place under the grill and melt the cheese for 3 minutes until golden and bubbling.

7 Carefully remove the dish from the grill and serve at the table for everyone to tuck in.

CREAMY ROASTED BUTTERNUT SQUASH & PIBS RISOTTO

This vibrant, creamy risotto is comfort food at its best and it is well worth the effort for its decadent flavour and velvety texture.

SERVES: 4
PREP TIME: 20 minutes
COOK TIME: 25 minutes

FOR THE BUTTERNUT

500g butternut squash, cut into 2cm cubes
1 tbsp rapeseed oil
1 tbsp smoked sweet paprika
sea salt and black pepper
10 The Jolly Hog Pigs in Blankets

FOR THE RISOTTO

1 tbsp salted butter
1 onion, finely diced
1 garlic clove, crushed
10 sage leaves, finely chopped, plus extra to serve
40ml dry white wine
1 vegetable stock cube
1.2 litres hot water
400g risotto rice
65g Parmesan, finely grated, plus extra to serve

TO SERVE

40g pine nuts, toasted
garlic bread

1 Preheat the oven to 200°C/180°C fan/gas mark 6.

2 Place the butternut squash cubes in a large roasting tin, sprinkle over the oil and paprika and season with salt and pepper. Add the pigs in blankets to the tray and roast for 20 minutes.

3 In the meantime, in a large pan, melt the butter over a medium heat and add the onion. Fry for 4–5 minutes until the onion starts to soften. Add the garlic, chopped sage and wine and bring to a simmer for 2 minutes.

4 Remove the squash and sausages from the oven and place half the cooked squash in a blender. Add the vegetable stock cube and the hot water and carefully blend.

5 Add the risotto rice to the pan and stir through the sage and onion mixture until well coated. Gradually add the butternut squash stock to the pan in intervals, ensuring all the liquid has been absorbed before adding more – this will take approximately 20–25 minutes.

6 When all the liquid has been absorbed and the rice is tender but still has a little bite, add the remaining roasted squash pieces. Chop the cooked pigs in blankets into small pieces and stir through the risotto along with the Parmesan.

7 Scatter over the toasted pine nuts, grated Parmesan and fresh sage and serve with garlic bread.

PIBS
THREE-CHEESE
TOASTIE

with Tomato Chutney

Why have one cheese when you can have three? Try our three-cheese toastie with lashings of sweet tomato chutney and punchy gherkins, and of course, stuffed full with pigs in blankets.

SERVES: 1
PREP TIME: 10 minutes
COOK TIME: 30 minutes

4 The Jolly Hog Pigs in Blankets
1 tbsp salted butter
2 thick slices of bread
2 tbsp tomato chutney
4 pickled gherkin slices
30g Cheddar and mozzarella, grated
20g Gruyère, grated
crisp green salad, to serve

You will need a toastie maker or sandwich press.

1 Preheat the oven to 200°C/180°C fan/gas mark 6.

2 Place the pigs in blankets in a roasting tin and roast in the oven for 25 minutes.

3 In the meantime, preheat a toastie maker or sandwich press while you prepare the sandwiches.

4 Butter one side of each slice of bread and place them butter-side down on a plate. Spread 1 tablespoon of chutney on each slice (on the unbuttered side) and lay the gherkin slices on one slice.

5 In a bowl mix together the grated cheeses and set aside.

6 When the sausages are cooked, place on top of the gherkins and top with the cheese.

7 Sandwich the two slices together so the buttered sides face outwards. Place the sandwich in the toastie maker of sandwich press and toast for 3–4 minutes until the cheese has melted inside and the bread is golden and toasted on the outside.

8 Slice in half and serve on a plate alongside a crisp green salad.

FOR THE PIZZA DOUGH

200g strong bread flour,
plus extra for dusting
3.5g fast-action yeast
pinch of sea salt
1 tbsp olive oil
110ml tepid water

FOR THE TOPPINGS

60g barbecue sauce
1 pepper, deseeded and
thinly sliced thinly
sliced
½ small red onion,
thinly sliced
10 The Jolly Hog Pigs
in Blankets, sliced
150g mozzarella ball
black pepper

Optional stand mixer
with a dough hook.

BBQ PIBS & PEPPER PIZZA

We all know and love
a barbecue take-away
pizza, so why not recreate
it at home but with the
addition of pack of
porky PIBS!

1 Preheat the oven to 220°C/200°C fan/gas mark 7.

2 Place the flour, yeast and salt in a bowl and create
a well. Pour in the oil along with the tepid water
and stir to roughly combine.

3 Knead the dough using a stand mixer fitted with
the dough hook attachment for 5–8 minutes or by
hand on a lightly floured surface for 8–10 minutes
until smooth and elastic. Cover with a clean tea
towel and set aside while you prepare the toppings.

4 Roll or press out the pizza dough to an
approximately 30cm-wide circle and place on
a lightly floured baking sheet.

5 Spoon on the barbecue sauce and spread over
the dough base leaving a 3cm border at the edge
of the dough. Sprinkle on the pepper and onion and
top with the sliced pigs in blankets. Roughly tear
the mozzarella ball and dot over the pizza.

6 Bake the pizza in the oven for 12–15 minutes
until the sausages are cooked through and the
crust is golden and crisp.

7 Slice and serve.

MAKES: 1 pizza
PREP TIME: 20 minutes
COOK TIME: 15 minutes

SALT & PEPPER PIBS

Already wrapped in deliciously salty bacon, pigs in blankets are brilliantly perfect for adding the salty kick to this Chinese-inspired dish.

SERVES: 2

PREP TIME: 5 minutes

COOK TIME: 10 minutes

1 tsp Sichuan peppercorns
1 tbsp cornflour
1 tsp five spice
10 The Jolly Hog Pigs in Blankets
1 tbsp sesame oil
2 pak choi
1 tbsp soy sauce
1 tbsp runny honey
1 tbsp sesame seeds, toasted

You will need a pestle and mortar.

1 Place the peppercorns in the mortar and grind until you have a fine powder. Place in a bowl along with the cornflour and five spice and stir to combine.

2 Place the pigs in blankets in the peppercorn powder and stir until all the sausages are coated.

3 Heat the sesame oil in a large wok over a medium-high heat. Add the sausages to the pan and fry for 4–5 minutes until crispy and golden.

4 Roughly chop the pak choi, but leave the central baby leaves whole, and add to the pan. Fry for 1 minute before adding the soy sauce and honey. Fry for a further 2 minutes.

5 When ready to serve, sprinkle over the toasted sesame seeds.

POSH PIBS FRY-UP TRAYBAKE

Make the ultimate lazy weekend treat by just throwing everything into a roasting tin and then the only thing you need to do is fry some eggs.

SERVES: 2
PREP TIME: 5 minutes
COOK TIME: 25 minutes

10 The Jolly Hog Pigs in Blankets
75g salted butter, softened
½ tbsp garlic puree
150g mushrooms, quartered
2 slices of white bread
2 tbsp rapeseed oil
150g vine tomatoes
sea salt and black pepper
2 medium free-range eggs
fresh parsley, roughly chopped, to serve

1 Preheat the oven to 200°C/180°C fan/gas mark 6.

2 Place the pigs in blankets in a large roasting tin and roast for 15 minutes.

3 Place the butter and the garlic puree in a bowl and add the mushrooms. Stir all the ingredients together to coat the mushrooms in the garlic butter.

4 In another bowl, tear the bread into 2–3cm size pieces and sprinkle with the oil. Toss the bread to completely coat in the oil.

5 After the sausages have been roasting for the 15 minutes, remove from the oven and turn. Add the garlic mushrooms, bread and vine tomatoes to the tray and season. Return to the oven for a further 10 minutes.

6 In the meantime, fry the eggs as desired.

7 Remove the tray from the oven, top with the fried eggs and sprinkle with a little freshly chopped parsley.

FOR THE POTATOES

400g potatoes
2 tbsp olive oil
10 The Jolly Hog Pigs
    in Blankets
sea salt and black pepper

FOR THE TOMATO SAUCE

2 tbsp olive oil
1 onion, chopped
1 garlic clove, finely
    chopped

1 x 400g tin chopped
    tomatoes
1 tbsp tomato puree
2 tsp sweet paprika
1 tsp chilli powder
1 tsp sugar

FOR THE CHEAT'S AIOLI

1 garlic clove, minced
1 tsp lemon juice
100g mayonnaise
1 tsp Dijon mustard

PIB-TATAS BRAVAS

A PIB-tastic twist on the Spanish classic, we've added our pigs in blankets, which go perfectly with the spicy tomato sauce and the garlicky aioli.

1 Preheat the oven to 200°C/180°C fan/gas mark 6.

2 Cut the potatoes into small cubes and put into a roasting tin with the oil and a good pinch of salt and pepper. Roast for 50 minutes until crisp and golden.

3 Whilst your potatoes are cooking, make the aioli and tomato sauce. Put the PIBs into another roasting tin and after 25 minutes add them to the same oven for 25 minutes.

4 To make the cheat's aioli, put the garlic in a bowl with the lemon juice and add a pinch of salt. Mix, then add the mayonnaise, mustard and a pinch of salt and pepper to taste.

5 To make the tomato sauce, heat the oil in a pan and add the onion and fry for 5 minutes until softened. Add the garlic, chopped tomatoes, tomato puree, paprika, chilli powder and sugar. Bring this mixture to the boil, stirring occasionally. Add a good pinch of salt and simmer for around 15 minutes until the sauce has thickened. Take off the heat and blend with a hand mixer until the sauce is smooth.

6 To assemble, tip the potatoes into a serving dish, top with the tomato sauce, drizzle with the cheat's aioli and top with PIBS.

SERVES: 4
PREP TIME: 30 minutes
COOK TIME: 50 minutes

AUTUMNAL PIBS GALETTE

with Squash & Apple

A super-quick, 'no-fuss' tart, this autumnal galette is a great way to celebrate the season. Sweet apple and squash work so well with our porky pigs in blankets.

SERVES: 4
PREP TIME: 5 minutes
COOK TIME: 25 minutes

150g cream cheese
75g blue cheese
black pepper
320g block of shortcrust
    pastry
flour, for dusting
6 slices of squash
1 apple, sliced
8 The Jolly Hog Pigs
    in Blankets

1 egg, lightly whisked
25g pecans
4 thyme sprigs, leaves
    picked

1 Preheat the oven to 200°C/180°C fan/gas mark 6. Line a baking tray with greaseproof paper.

2 In a bowl, combine the cream cheese, blue cheese and a crack of black pepper.

3 Roll the pastry out on a lightly floured surface, cut into a roughly 30cm-diameter circle and place on the lined baking tray.

4 Spread the cream cheese mixture on the pastry circle leaving a 3cm border. Add the squash and apple slices on top of the cheese, then place the pigs in blankets on top.

5 Fold up the side of the pastry to roughly enclose the tart and form the classic round galette shape. Brush the pastry edges with the whisked egg and bake in the oven for 20 minutes.

6 Remove the galette from the oven, sprinkle over the pecans and return to the oven for a final 5 minutes until the galette is golden and crisp and the pecans are toasted.

7 Remove from the oven, sprinkle with a fresh thyme leaves and serve.

MINI PIBS
MAC 'N' CHEESE
POTS

Combining Cheddar, mozzarella and Gruyère, these cheesy pasta pots are made even better with the addition of little piggies! Made in advance and baked in the oven when ready to serve makes these a hassle-free dinner any day of the week.

MAKES: 4
PREP TIME: 10 minutes
COOK TIME: 45 minutes

200g macaroni pasta
1 tbsp sunflower oil
10 The Jolly Hog Pigs
  in Blankets, diced
3 spring onions, finely
  chopped
1 garlic clove, crushed
50g salted butter
50g plain flour
650ml milk
100g grated Cheddar
  and mozzarella, grated
75g Gruyère, grated
25g salt and pepper
  crisps

TO SERVE
fresh parsley, roughly
  chopped
garlic bread

You will need 4 large,
  ovenproof ramekins.

1 Preheat the oven to 200°C/180°C fan/gas mark 6.

2 Pour the pasta into a pan of boiling, salted water and cook until just al dente – approximately 2 minutes short of the cook time on the packet instruction. Drain and set aside.

3 Heat the oil in a large pan and add the sausages and spring onions. Fry for 4–5 minutes until the sausages begin to brown. Add the garlic and fry for a further 1 minute before removing the pan from the heat.

4 In a clean, heavy-bottomed saucepan, melt the butter over a medium heat. Whisk in the flour and cook for 1 minute, whisking continuously to ensure it does not burn.

5 Gradually add the milk to the roux, whisking all the time until you have a smooth, glossy sauce. Add all the cheeses and whisk until completely melted.

6 Add the drained pasta to the pan with the cheese sauce and stir in until well until combined, and divide the cheesy pasta into four ramekin dishes.

7 Place the crisps in a bowl and crush using the end of a rolling pin, then sprinkle on the top of each pasta pot. Place the ramekins in a roasting tin and put in the oven to bake for 15–20 minutes until golden and bubbling.

8 Finish with a sprinkling of roughly chopped parsley and serve with garlic bread for dipping.

1 tbsp rapeseed oil
1 red onion, finely diced
1 celery stick, finely diced
1 carrot, diced
1 large garlic clove, crushed
sea salt
10 The Jolly Hog Pigs in Blankets, snipped into small chunks using scissors
100ml good-quality red wine
250g dried red lentils, rinsed and drained

1 tbsp sun-dried tomato paste
½ tbsp smoked paprika
500ml vegetable or meat stock, or more if needed
2 x 400g tins chopped tomatoes
1 tbsp maple syrup or soft brown sugar

TO SERVE
spaghetti for 6
grated Parmesan
fresh basil leaves

PIBS & LENTIL BOLOGNESE

Sausage meat is a great way to add flavour to a lentil-based ragu, and mini sausages wrapped in salty bacon are even better!

1 Heat the oil in a large pan over a medium heat. Add the onion, celery and carrot and gently fry for 4–5 minutes until it begins to soften. Add the garlic along with a generous pinch of salt and continue to fry for 2 minutes.

2 Add the snipped pigs in blankets to the pan. Fry for 3–4 minutes until the sausages start to brown. Add the wine to deglaze the pan and simmer for 2 minutes.

3 Add the drained lentils to the pan along with the tomato paste and paprika. Stir to thoroughly combine all the ingredients.

4 Pour in the stock, tomatoes and maple syrup or sugar and bring to the boil. Turn down the heat and allow to gently simmer for 30 minutes, occasionally stirring to ensure the lentils do not stick. If the lentils absorb all the liquid, simply add a little more stock. Season to taste.

5 When nearly ready to serve, cook the pasta in a pan of boiling salted water according to the packet instructions. Drain the pasta, divide between four to six bowls and top with the lentil ragu.

6 Finish each dish with a grating of Parmesan and some fresh basil.

SERVES: 4–6*
PREP TIME: 10 minutes
COOK TIME: 45 minutes
* for 6 served with spaghetti, for 4 served without

101

'MUMMY'S' HALLOWEEN PIBS

Give everyone a fright this Halloween with these pastry-wrapped pigs-in-blankets mummies. Great for a haunting Halloween party or a terrifying tea-time treat.

MAKES: 20
PREP TIME: 10 minutes
COOK TIME: 25 minutes

FOR THE MUMMIES
500g block of puff pastry
10 The Jolly Hog Pigs in Blankets
1 egg, lightly whisked

FOR THE DECORATION
50g cream cheese
5 black pitted olives
tomato ketchup, for dipping

1 Preheat the oven to 200°C/180°C fan/gas mark 6. Line a baking tray with greaseproof paper.

2 Roll out the pastry and cut into 5mm wide, long strips and wrap around each sausage in a disorderly fashion to give the impression of rough bandages, leaving a small space at the top of each sausage for the eyes.

3 Place the wrapped pigs in blankets on the lined baking tray and brush each sausage with a little whisked egg. Bake in the oven for 25 minutes until the pastry is golden brown.

4 Remove the pigs in blankets from the oven and allow to cool before decorating.

5 Either using a piping bag or simply a small spoon, add two cream cheese eyes to each mummy. Chop the olives into very small pieces and place one piece on each cream cheese blob to become the blacks of the eyes.

6 Transfer to a serving plate alongside some tomato ketchup for dipping.

INDEX

Note: page numbers in **bold** refer to illustrations.

110

ACKNOWLEDGEMENTS

On behalf of Max, Josh and myself, I would like to say a huge thank you to lots of people who have helped make this happen. Firstly, to our suppliers and the retailers we work with. To Liv, Harriet, Chesk and the whole Hog HQ team for being the driving force behind this wonderful celebration of pigs in blankets. Lastly to our family who have been on this Jolly journey with us through thick and thin (not referring to waistlines or hairlines!). Mum, Dad, Ella, Claire, Kate, Mark and Will. Here's to sharing more Jolly Good moments of JOY!

Olly
Ps – please remember that PIBs aren't just for Christmas, they are for life!

111

Ebury Press an imprint of Ebury Publishing,
20 Vauxhall Bridge Road,
London SW1V 2SA

Ebury Press is part of the Penguin Random House group
of companies whose addresses can be found at global.
penguinrandomhouse.com

First published by Ebury Press in 2022

www.penguin.co.uk

A CIP catalogue record for this book is available from
the British Library

ISBN 9781529902389

Printed and Bound in the UK by Bell & Bain Ltd

Recipe Writer and Food Stylist: Helen Upshall
Photography: Josh Campbell
Project Editors: Olivia Bennett and Francesca Fox
Cover and book design: maru studio
Production: Rebecca Jones
Publisher: Elizabeth Bond

The authorised representative in the EEA is Penguin
Random House Ireland, Morrison Chambers, 32 Nassau
Street, Dublin D02 YH68

Penguin Random House is committed to a
sustainable future for our business, our readers
and our planet. This book is made from Forest
Stewardship Council® certified paper.